Chiricahua Mountains

Gregory McNamee, SERIES EDITOR

For Mark —

hoping you enjoy this
wild place in AZ!

Chiricahua Mountains

Bridging the Borders of Wildness

[signature]

TEXT BY Ken Lamberton

PHOTOGRAPHS BY Jeff Garton

The University of Arizona Press   Tucson

The University of Arizona Press
© 2003 Ken Lamberton
First Printing
All rights reserved

∞ This book is printed on acid-free, archival-quality paper.
Manufactured in the United States of America

08 07 06 05 04 03   6 5 4 3 2 1

Library of Congress Cataloging-in-Publication Data appear on the last
printed page of this book.

British Library Cataloguing-in-Publication Data
A catalogue record for this book is available from the British Library.

Frontispiece: Road into the southern Chiricahuas

For SALLY HOYT SPOFFORD
1914–2002

contents

photographs

PHOTOGRAPHS
xii

acknowledgments

First, I wish to thank Peter Barnes and the Common Counsel Foundation for two glorious weeks at the Mesa Refuge in Point Reyes Station, California, where I finished this book in the presence of fog-draped pines and barn swallows. *Mi casa es su casa*. And to Chuck LaRue, who patiently obliged my desert legs and lungs, your companionship and expertise are invaluable to me. To my community of writers—Richard Shelton, Alison Deming, Fenton Johnson, Alan Weisman, Madeline Kiser, Marilyn Snell, Daniel Gold, Marilyn Sewell—and to the Río Nuevo Writer's Group who read and commented on these words: Tony Luebbermann, Deidre Elliott, Mac Hudson, Josh

Cohn, Spring Ulmer, David Murchison, Ralph Hager, my sincerest gratitude and appreciation. Where would I be without all of you in my life? Furthermore, where would this book be without the many behind-the-scenes researchers and naturalists upon whose work it depends? Janice Emily Bowers, David E. Brown, Charles Cole, Alden Hayes, Richard Taylor—to name only a few. I am grateful for you all. To Jeff Garton, photographer and friend—my words hardly do justice to your exquisite images. And finally, to my editors and friends Greg McNamee and Patti Hartmann at the University of Arizona Press, thank you both for your encouragement and advice, and for your support of this project.

K. L.

Chiricahua Mountains

Volcanic hoodoos south of Massai Point, Chiricahua National Monument

orogeny

As a rule, I generally jump at opportunities to blow out my knees. So when I heard someone had spotted a pair of short-tailed hawks in the Chiricahua Mountains, I figured I'd be climbing some wicked mountain switchbacks to see the birds for myself. Although I enjoy bird-watching, I've never before rushed off anywhere in response to a rare bird report. Well, at least not like some of the more fanatical bird-watchers I know. Recently, several British "birders," after getting an email alert about white-eared hummingbirds in the Chiricahuas, flew to southeast Arizona, drove a rental car up the mountains, and camped out near a single clump of blooming penstemon the hummingbirds had been frequenting—all to place one more check mark on a so-called "life list." I probably won't travel that far for a humming-bird. But I do have a certain fascination with raptors—those birds of prey at the apex of the biomass pyramid, like hawks, falcons, and eagles—particularly the uncommon species. Short-tailed hawks are small, crow-sized, tropical broad-winged raptors that normally range from Mexico to South America. They inhabit mountainous regions and mixed woodlands and are very rare north of the border. Less than five hundred birds cross into the United States, some in Texas and more in Florida. Only a few years ago, they were hypothetical in Arizona.

Hypothetical. According to birder vernacular, *hypothetical* birds are species that haven't yet made it from bush to hand. Only a few sight records—by competent and experienced orni-thologists—exist, not specimens or "distinguishable parts thereof." They are like ghosts, tangible and intangible at the same time. The 1981 *Annotated Checklist of the Birds of Arizona* has no listing for short-tailed hawks. My 1991 edition of *The Audubon Society Encyclopedia of North American Birds* says that this Mexi-can and Central and South American species reaches the United States only in Florida where it is "rare and local." *The Sibley Guide to Birds,* published in 2000, shows a green dot in southeastern Arizona representing a location of "rare occurrence" for short-tailed hawks. A *single* green dot.

The first "hypothetical" sighting of short-tailed hawks in Ari-zona happened on August 7, 1985, at Barfoot Junction in the Chiricahua Mountains. John Arvin, a bird-watcher and naturalist, was leading a tour in the Chiricahuas as he had been doing regularly during the spring and summer seasons. He'd also been taking people south of Sonora, Mexico, to Sinaloa and Nayarit where he often saw the hawks. "But I had no idea that there were any short-tailed hawks any closer to Arizona than extreme southern Sonora," he explained in a letter to me. Around midday, he and his group were just returning to the van after an excursion on foot. "I saw the bird coming through breaks in the trees and I realized it was either a short-tailed hawk or a white-tailed hawk because of its extensive white underparts and dark, helmet-like head." John Arvin knew about records of white-tailed hawks in southeast Arizona, and this is what he expected to identify. He alerted his group and concentrated on an opening in the trees overhead where the hawk would appear; when it did, he followed the bird carefully, noting every feature before it disappeared behind a nearby ridge. "I immediately sat down with a notebook and recorded all my impressions while they were fresh in my mind. Some of the group hadn't seen this technique of documenting rare sightings immediately in the field instead of running to the books for look-alike comparisons with pictures." Going over these notes, John Arvin realized that he hadn't seen a white-tailed hawk. Instead, he'd seen a hawk that no one had ever seen before in Arizona.

By 1998, when the Arizona Bird Committee (a group of elected bird-watchers that maintains and evaluates rare bird reports) published an update of the official state list of bird species, only two additional sightings of short-tailed hawks existed, one from the nearby Huachuca Mountains on July 21, 1988, and another from the Chiricahuas on March 7, 1990. Although the committee believed the reports, it would not accept John Arvin's or the following two sightings "without some additional form of physical evidence." The birds remained ghosts, hypothetical ghosts.

Then in 1999, Gary Rosenberg, secretary of the Arizona Bird Committee, photographed the hawk in the Huachucas, establishing the first documented proof of a short-tailed hawk in Arizona. The following year, the committee increased the official state list by seven new species, one of them the short-tailed hawk, bringing the total number of birds recorded in Arizona to 522.

Still, these hawks remain enigmatic, which fascinates me. Although the birds have become official for Arizona, few people have seen them. Those who have, find them mostly in the Chiricahuas near 8,823-foot Barfoot Lookout. No one yet, however, knows whether the hawks are reproducing in Arizona, but some people suspect that they are. Rick Taylor, master birdwatcher and probably the best authority on birds in the Chiricahuas, is one of those who believes they are breeding here. Rick Taylor, in fact, was the instigation for my trip to the Chiricahuas. His was the latest sighting of shorttails: "I had a pair for forty-five minutes on the north slope of Buena Vista Peak at the cattle guard," he told my longtime friend and hiking compadre Chuck LaRue. "One bird was so motionless as it hovered overhead that I actually put it in the scope. When it would float out of sight, I'd simply move the scope one degree or less to center on the bird again."

Based on this sighting and his own recent observations,

Chuck LaRue was certain the hawks were courting. When he asked me to join him on a trip to the Chiricahua high country to search for nesting short-tailed hawks, I enthusiastically accepted. I wanted to know what attracted these hawks to this isolated backlot in our state. What did they "see" in this wilderness?

I first met Chuck in 1983 when he worked as an environmental scientist for a company in northern Arizona. He was raised and educated in the Four Corners region, having attended the Navajo Reservation's Bureau of Indian Affairs (BIA) schools (although he is not Native American) and then Northern Arizona University. His years of doing wildlife inventories on the Colorado Plateau have made him an expert regional naturalist, specializing in birds. For the last few years, Chuck has been living in Flagstaff and working as a freelance consultant biologist around the state. His most recent job entailed monitoring ferruginous pygmy owls in an area near the new Ironwood National Monument, north of Tucson. During that visit, he called me with Rick Taylor's news of the short-tailed hawks and we began planning our excursion to the Chiricahuas.

Growing up in Tucson, I often traveled to this "sky island" tucked into the far southeastern corner of Arizona. Every time I visited there, the mountains rewarded me for my budding devotion to its landscape. These rewards—gifts really, because they seemed to come not from my own efforts but by grace—might have been a blurred hawkmoth sipping from a moonlit datura bloom or a tree-splitting detonation in a lightning storm. Both

Datura blooms

could be just as hair-raising. I felt I hardly deserved the pleasure the place stirred in me.

To many people, the name Chiricahuas is synonymous with birds, particularly subtropical specialties such as zebra-faced Mexican chickadees, painted redstarts, and the prized trogon with the coppery tail—reason enough to make the trip. But what originally drew me to the mountains was their remote border-land location. The Chiricahuas comprise the largest single range in southern Arizona, yet there are no paved roads crisscrossing them. In some places there are no roads at all, only three hundred plus miles of trails. Although wilderness in any context, geographical or emotional, moves me, I'm attracted to life that exists at the edge. These mountains, as with any oceanic island, are a marginal place; here plants and animals either adapt or they go extinct. David Quammen, in *The Song of the Dodo: Island Biogeography in an Age of Extinction,* calls geographical isolation "the flywheel of evolution." The Chiricahuas have this kind of inertia, a persistent motion that sustains the relic species while rapidly separating and transforming others more responsive. In these mountains I can expect anything, even the unexpected, because life is also most abundant at the edge.

To understand the Chiricahuas' rich diversity of plants and animals, one must understand the mountain range's origins. Geologists say that a wild frenzy of volcanic activity about twenty-seven million years ago created much of the Chiricahua Mountains we see today. Thick jackets of volcanic ash, between 120 and 240 cubic miles from at least eight successive eruptions, covered the entire central mountain area. The Turkey Creek Caldera, a collapsed magma chamber and remnant of the volcanic episode, may have once reached nearly 13 miles across before other eruptions obscured it. Ida, Sentinel, and Buena Vista Peaks sketch a quarter circle of the caldera's leftover rim.

In the 16 square miles of Chiricahua National Monument at the north end of the range, erosion has exposed thousands of feet of this volcanic ash, compacted into a rock called "tuff." What was once hot, gas-charged ash and pumice laid down in incandescent flows and fused together into "welded" and "unwelded" tuffs from two to almost nine hundred feet thick, has weathered into curious rock formations. Like a stadium full of petrified spectators, crowds of these weird spires, columns, and totem poles seem poised in some eternal moment of ovation.

Visitors can view the most bizarre of these "hoodoos" along the Bonita Canyon road to Massai Point, named for the Apache scout "Bigfoot" Massai, who, as the story goes, mysteriously appeared among these standing rocks years after Geronimo's capture. The hoodoos take fanciful shapes—from people to cartoon characters to fungus. There's Praying Padre, Ugly Duckling, China Boy with his coolie hat, the Bishop wearing his miter, and others that rise from the imagination. The rocks are the color and texture of dry bread. Moldlike smudges in muted gray-greens, yellows, and blacks garnish the rough surfaces and enhance color and texture. The smudges are lichens, primitive associations of fungi and algae that munch mountains into sediments and only grow inches in a century. In the monument and throughout the Chiricahuas, lichens gnaw on impressive galleries of towers, turrets, obelisks, natural bridges, and balanced rocks.

What formed the Chiricahuas, however, wasn't just this brief cataclysmic episode but the much longer period of regional mountain building that followed. Between fifteen and eight million years ago, a second kind of geologic upheaval took over—basalt volcanism. Unlike rhyolite volcanoes that erupt violently, basalt volcanoes spread lava across valley floors like spilled syrup on a tabletop. Rhyolite lava, composed largely of silica, is infused with gases under pressure making it explosive; basalt lava has less gas. It's like the difference between Kilauea and Mount St. Helens. Kilauea you run toward when it erupts; you run from Mount St. Helens.

This period initiated the Basin and Range landscape of the West that we see today. This is a landscape formed by eight million years of rising mountains and sinking valleys, the latter of which is still going on today near the Chiricahuas. As tectonic forces began stretching and pulling apart the earth's crust, hundreds of long, narrow "fault block" ranges, which slash obliquely northwest to southeast from southern Oregon and Idaho through Nevada and across the lower half of Arizona into northeastern Mexico, separated from wide basins. The basins sank and eventually, over millions of years of erosion, filled with mountain debris. Thousands of feet of gravel, sand, and clay now pack these basins, along whose margins rise the familiar mountains of southern Arizona's skyline: the Rincons, Santa

Ritas, Santa Catalinas, Huachucas, and Chiricahuas. This is the Basin and Range Province, and there's no other place like it on the planet.

As if the Chiricahuas were part of an archipelago drained of its ocean, this, the largest of the sky islands, is one link in a chain of mountains connecting the Rockies to the Sierra Madre Occidental in Mexico. Many plants and animals in the Chiricahuas have their centers of origin and diversity in the Sierra Madres. Some of these "Madrean" species even reach the northernmost extension of their ranges here: birds like elegant trogons and sulphur-bellied flycatchers, mammals like jaguarundis and Chiricahua fox squirrels, and trees like the Apache pine. But the Rocky Mountains also have an influence in the Chiricahuas. For example, at the highest elevations in the range, on the north- and east-facing slopes of Chiricahua Peak, grow the southernmost stands of Engelmann spruce in North America.

Also, at the Chiricahuas' northeast shoulder, the Chihuahuan Desert leans against the mountains, resulting in an abrupt mingling of woodland and desert habitats. This, together with the proximity of the Sonoran Desert to the west, affects the complexion of the range's wildlife (both flora and fauna). Riparian drainages bisect these mountain slopes, grasslands, and desert flats to create natural corridors. A few of these streams, like the ones in the southeast corner of the range that spill into the San Bernardino Valley, which in turn drains into the Rio Yaqui, connect the Chiricahuas to wildlife originating in the Sinaloan thorn forest four hundred miles away in Mexico.

Then there's the physical profile of the mountains themselves. Because an increase in elevation means an increase in moisture and a decrease in temperature, in southern Arizona every one thousand feet upslope equals about four additional inches of precipitation annually and an average four-degree-Fahrenheit drop in temperature. The higher one climbs, the more temperate the climate and the more temperate the species. In cross-section, this vertical arrangement of wildlife illustrates a kind of natural environment graduated into what C. Hart Merriam at the turn of last century called "life zones."

Merriam's life zone scheme isn't perfect, and many biologists have refined it to the more comprehensive "biotic community" model. Still, other scientists recognize the concept's usefulness, particularly in western landscapes. Ecologist Charles Lowe argues that despite shortcomings, Merriam's classification system endures as a tool because it is simple and straightforward, and because it works. It still remains one of the most graphic ways of showing plant and animal diversity in places like the Chiricahuas. From desert valley to highest peak, the mountains climb through five of Merriam's six life zones for Arizona, encompassing varied lowland, foothill, canyon, and mountain communities.

From San Simon Valley in the northeast one traverses the Lower Sonoran life zone of the Chihuahuan Desert, a dry flatland of wrought-iron mesquite, spidery ocotillo, dusty creosote and tarbush, kangaroo rats, and diamondback rattlesnakes, with its associated birds: Inca doves, scaled quail, roadrunners, and power pole sentries like Swainson's hawks and Chihuahuan ravens. Ascending into the Chiricahua Mountains from Portal, one enters the Upper Sonoran life zone (above 4,000 feet) where the stalks of yucca, century plant, and desert spoon stab the skyline and spiny lizards and catlike ringtails mix with Montezuma quail and burrowing owls. Continuing into the Upper Sonoran life zone of Cave Creek Canyon, past Steward Campground and the Southwestern Research Station at about 5,400 feet, oak-pine woodlands and streamside groves of sycamore and walnut offer shelter for coatimundis, Chiricahua fox squirrels, and canyon treefrogs as well as nesting sites for zone-tailed hawks, whiskered screech-owls, and elegant trogons. Entering black bear country of the Arizona and ponderosa pine forests above 6,000 feet around East Turkey Creek and on toward Onion Saddle, the diligent observer might catch glimpses of blushing hepatic tanagers and red-faced warblers, or hear the evening rhythmic songs of whip-poor-wills and flammulated owls. Also, spotted owls bark out their territories here, in the deep-forested ravines of Merriam's Transition life zone. Even farther up, near an elevation of 8,000 feet, aspen groves and forests of Douglas and white fir characterize the Canadian zone. At Rustler and Barfoot Parks, one might find twin-spotted rattlesnakes coiled among the pink rocks of the talus slopes, or Mexican chickadees and hermit thrushes trilling and fluting from the trees while violet-green swallows glide above them on razor wings. And finally, where Engelmann spruce appear on the highest peaks, around 9,000 feet above sea level in the Hudsonian life zone, red-breasted nuthatches and golden-crowned kinglets hang beak-down from bark perches. Weather permitting (and it usually is),

Darnell Peak, eastern Chiricahuas (from San Simon Valley)

Detail of century plant

an energetic bird-watcher venturing into the Chiricahuas can explore the ranges of hundreds of species of birds in a single day.

The Chiricahua Mountains are a bird-watcher's utopia . . . and more. The whole extraordinary geographical arrangement—the bridge between mountain ranges and border between deserts, the riparian drainages and life zone profile—creates a conjunction of biological communities unlike anywhere else in North America. The Chiricahuas are more than a holy place for birders. They are a nature watcher's Mecca: A place where one connects to the landscape, to the story of life.

Clouds over West Turkey Creek

west turkey creek

Chuck and I approach the Chiricahua Mountains from the west by way of Sulphur Springs Valley. The valley, twenty-five miles wide and stretching about a hundred miles north and south, flanks the entire western portion of the range. We take Highway 191, skirting the margin of Willcox Playa, to Highway 181 and the farming community of Sunizona. Our destination, and tonight's camping spot, is the large, stream-creased canyon of West Turkey Creek.

Agriculture in Sulphur Springs Valley produces a variety of crops, from apples to alfalfa, corn, cotton, and chilies. Farmers owe the fertility of the valley to rich sediments left behind by

Lake Cochise, a Pleistocene freshwater lake that about twelve thousand years ago filled over eighty square miles of the inter-mountain basin. Today, most of what remains of Lake Cochise are the grasslands and stabilized dune fields of its ancient shore-line and a blinding plain of potassium, calcium, and sodium carbonate crust now called Willcox Playa. Because the playa has no outlet, seasonal rains collect there and sometimes form a broad, inches-deep lake that the sun slowly dries into layers of alkaline deposits, as has been happening for thousands of years.

This combination of playa and plow attracts sandhill cranes to Sulphur Springs Valley each winter. Before the 1950s the birds were unheard of here, although the area had much to offer the four-foot-tall, russet-capped, gray-feathered, gregarious migrant that's all legs, neck, and beak: mild climate, shallow standing water, and open grassy roosts. Then farmers began planting corn, milo, sorghum, winter wheat, and oats. In 1960, a few cranes ventured into the valley from a population in New Mexico, and the pioneers discovered October fields of harvested grains. The following year more cranes arrived. Then more. That decade, every fall, starting about the last week in September, the cranes came. The first Arizona Game and Fish Department survey in 1970 counted 750 birds. In the winter of 1978–79, they numbered more than 5,000. The next winter, 2,000 more joined these. It appeared as though the sandhills had found a new winter home. But in the 1980s, a drought-induced decline in irrigated agricul-ture and a sinking water table cut the population in half. The sandhill cranes at Willcox Playa, who had won the hearts of the local residents, needed help.

Today, farmers plant mostly corn and chilies—the stubble-fields of which the cranes relish—rather than former crops like winter wheat and oats. Also, the Arizona Game and Fish Department pumps water into protected ponds on the playa that the cranes can use for roosting, regardless of weather conditions. Since 1996, the yearly census of sandhills at Willcox Playa has numbered better than 20,000 birds; wildlife officials are confident that the population is stable and secure.

"We have a lot more going on than just cranes," the people behind "Wings Over Willcox" like to say. The annual festival in the third week of January, sponsored by the Willcox Chamber of Commerce, offers food, craft shows, birding tours, and free natural history seminars. And people, like the cranes, come in flocks. The whole program is visionary, not only in its economics and environmentalism but in the way that *wildlife* is part of a community of caring farmers, ranchers, and business people. The sandhill crane issue at Willcox could have been purely ecological: the importance of creating population reservoirs and sustaining wildlife diversity. Or it could have been economical: wildlife means tourists, which equals dollars. But the primary issue of the cranes seems to be as basic as affection. Affection, too, should have standing. It makes sense to work toward the health of species simply because we value their place in our lives.

Wendell Berry says that we do not live alone. "Living is a communal act, whether or not its communality is acknowledged." We have a responsibility to each other, to all life that shares space with us on the planet, whether we inhabit cities or homestead roadless regions. The neighborhood is global. And living connects us to wilderness in one way or another. The challenge will be learning to share our world—our cities and rural communities, even our designated wilderness areas—with the new immigrants, the borderless ones with wings and song as well as the ones red in tooth and claw.

We stop at a bridge crossing West Turkey Creek near where the stream leaks out of the mountains through an encinal woodland. (*Encinal* is Spanish for "place of live oaks.") The morning air is already heavy and warm, which is typical for early May. Mesquite trees along the hillsides droop with yellow catkins. Dust as fine as puffball spores dulls the hard green leaves of the roadside Emory oak. In the creek, however, water is moving, and the willow and sycamore trees lining the banks take advantage of it. Below the bridge, two black phoebes flutter about, snatching unseen insects with audible clicks.

In the dust at the right side of the dirt road, Chuck points out the trackway of a very large cat. "Mountain lion," he says. "Came this way earlier this morning."

I think: *This is going to be an amazing four days.*

West Turkey Creek was my idea. I knew that Chuck would just as soon get into the high country to stake out a place to watch for short-tailed hawks. But I had never visited West Turkey Creek, whose dilating canyons and their tributaries spread across the western flank of the mountains like a five-fingered sycamore leaf. These canyons—Saulsbury, Ward, Mormon, Morse, and Pole Bridge—reach to the highest peaks of the range, and drain enough of the watershed from the crest of the mountains to provide permanent water except during the worst droughts. The perennial streams, together with the nightly rivers of cold air coursing down-canyon with them, support the Chiricahuas' heaviest stands of pines. Loggers once worked a sawmill here in the late 1800s to feed the hunger for raw timber of mining towns like Bisbee and Tombstone.

We park at Sycamore Campground where lichen-crusted boulders stud the dry bed of Turkey Creek. Birdsong and wind curl through a mixed woodland of oak and pine. Netleaf oaks patch the hillsides, browning and dropping leaves, but the pines appear robust in their dense clutches of dark green needles. We see Chihuahua pine, with its short two- to four-inch needles in bundles of threes and its doorknob-sized cones, as well as the less common Apache pine (so named because its range roughly matches that of the original Apache inhabitants here). Both evergreens occur only in southeast Arizona, southwest New Mexico, and in the mountains of northern Mexico.

Under wind-flashing silverleaf oaks, blue lupines bloom at the roadside, mocking the heat and drought. Bloody-stemmed manzanita already have green, marble-sized fruits, which pucker my lips when I press one between my teeth. The squawbush also have a few red, dried, and tart berries unclaimed by the campground chipmunks.

This is a classic Madrean Evergreen Woodland, specifically the Mexican oak-pine woodland, a biotic community that tends to tongue down cooler canyons in the Chiricahuas. In C. Hart Merriam's classification system, this 6,000-foot elevation corresponds to the Upper Sonoran life zone. However, since the Upper Sonoran life zone also includes various grasslands, chaparral, and oak woodlands, the limitations of the life zone system become apparent. David E. Brown, a biology professor at Arizona State University and the editor of the definitive guide *Biotic Communities: Southwestern United States and Northwestern Mexico,* says that one advantage of the biotic community approach is that these communities are easily recognized and even mapped on the basis of certain "indicator" species. For example, Chihuahua and Apache pine, together with netleaf and silverleaf oak, are indicators of the Mexican oak-pine woodland, whereas Emory, Mexican blue, and Arizona white oak with pinyon pine and alligator juniper characterize the encinal woodland. Both are subunits of the Madrean Evergreen Woodland. The biotic community system also relies on indicator animals as well as plants, including rare and endangered species. In addition to elevation, it takes into account nonliving elements like soil properties and landform history. The entire classification hierarchy is flexible. Ecologists may add new units and combine or delete old ones as further research indicates.

I notice that the pines, the sycamores, and most of the oaks seem immune to lichen infestations. In lime-greens and sky-grays, the raised-relief maps of lichens mottle only the silverleaf oaks (and the rocks), although other trees may grow adjacent to them. Do lichens have taste preferences? Sunlight lays against my skin where I sit on a lichen-stuccoed boulder writing notes. Chuck has followed the birdsong farther down stream, answering the bird notes with his own repertoire of squeaks, *psshes*, and owl calls. I haven't learned the language. Instead, I listen, mistaking the *kekking* of a northern flicker for a Cooper's hawk, as Dopplering flies circle my head, and then alight to crawl over my hands, legs, and notebook.

Later in the afternoon, Chuck suggests that we hike up Morse Canyon trail, a four-mile climb to Morse Saddle that features switchbacks and a 2,000-foot elevation gain in the final two miles. Wearing his khaki ball cap, T-shirt, blue jeans, and Nike hiking shoes, he leads the way. I follow with worried knees, knowing he has short-tailed hawks on his mind.

We follow an old logging road alongside a dry creek, our feet crunching on explosively brittle pine duff. The oak and pine canopy keeps us in shade and screens out even the wind, making the sound of our footfalls hang around our ears. The woodland seems an appropriate place to encounter creatures with strange names like hermit thrush, brown creeper, elf owl, and coatimundi. I've heard that bands of coatis, racoonlike animals with long snouts and erect, woolly-monkey tails, forage among the canyons of Turkey Creek and a few other wooded canyons of the isolated sky islands in southeastern Arizona, their northernmost range, which apparently is still expanding. Observers first noticed the animals north of the border in the nearby Huachuca Mountains in 1892; no one had recorded them in the Chiricahuas until 1929. Since the animals forage during the day, I'm watching for them.

Where the road tapers into trail near a grove of aspen, Chuck suddenly shouts "goshawk!" and immediately the woodland fills with the sound of his deep, throaty great horned owl imitation. Startled, I catch sight of a large gray hawk sliding through the trees and shadows before it vanishes. "Damn!" he says, and continues calling a few more times. "Did you see her? If she had a nest nearby, she'd respond. I think she's gone."

I've had goshawks on my list of birds to see since I began anticipating this trip to the Chiricahuas. I'd seen sharp-shinned hawks before, and, in Tucson, Cooper's hawks, even within urban areas like city parks, where the hawks have recently begun nesting. But goshawks, the largest of the short-winged, bird-hunting, accipiter clan, are new for me. I knew the likelihood of encountering goshawks here was great. The predators gave Noel Snyder trouble in the late 1980s and early 1990s when he was trying to reintroduce thick-billed parrots to the Chiricahua Mountains.

Less than a century ago, thick-billed parrots, raucous, bright-green birds with heavy beaks for feasting on pine cones, ranged from the Sierra Madre Occidental northward to central Arizona's Verde Valley. Photographs taken in the early 1900s show wagons loaded with dead parrots, like chickens on the way to market. Other photos depict soldiers posed with their rifles and laden with the day's kill. The parrots were easy targets for hunters and popular as food in many burgeoning mining towns. This, coupled with a loss of habitat as loggers cut trees to supply fuel for smelters and wood for construction, soon caused the extirpation of thickbills north of Mexico. Before Noel Snyder's program, the last reports of thick-billed parrots in Arizona came out of Rhyolite Canyon in Chiricahua National Monument in 1938.

Noel, who lives with his wife, Helen, in the town of Portal on the eastern side of the Chiricahuas, began working with the Arizona Game and Fish Department in 1986 to reestablish thick-billed parrots to their former home in the region. He'd had experience with parrots as a biologist with the Patuxent Center in Maryland where, from 1973 to 1976, he worked with the endangered Puerto Rican parrot.

Years ago, Noel Snyder told me about his difficulties reintroducing extirpated thick-billed parrots to southeastern Arizona. "There was lots of exploratory behavior," he said about his first release in the fall of 1986. "Their range spread out to different mountains, and there wasn't much we could do to track them." Snyder's team had discovered that these wild-caught parrots, confiscated from poachers who had brought them across the border to supply an illegal pet trade, had nomadic proclivities. The following summer, after goshawks killed seven birds and eight flew back to Mexico, a remnant flock of fourteen parrots traveled halfway across the state to the Mogollon Rim. They remained there, feeding among the pine and fir trees until September when, nearly a year after their return to the wild, the birds completed their migratory cycle by flying back to the Chiricahua Mountains.

This migration pattern continued in 1988. Bolstered with additional releases, the parrots again spent the summer in Mogollon Rim country and the winter in the Chiricahuas, this time returning to the release site in November with two untagged birds—pale-billed juveniles! For the first time in fifty years, thick-billed parrots had reproduced in Arizona. Unfortunately, these two offspring would be the only successes of the reintroduction program.

Although using wild-caught thickbills presented some problems, Noel Snyder found that they performed better after release than captive-bred, hand-reared parrots. Wild birds formed cohesive flocks, located more food by foraging over larger areas, and avoided predators by posting sentries—all social skills that captive-bred parrots lacked. Captive-reared parrots, however, were more readily available and disease-free. Snyder's greatest task involved finding ways to use both kinds of parrots, ideally releasing captive-bred parrots into a previously socially competent, wild-caught flock so that the inept birds might learn from their peers before something ate them.

But events beyond Snyder's control proved too much of a challenge. In 1989, three nests failed due to predators, and a drought devastated the pine crop in the less-diversified conifer forest of the Mogollon Rim. Then, the Dude Fire of 1990 destroyed the flock's summer range. Only a few parrots managed to return to the Chiricahuas that fall, which goshawks soon finished off. Undaunted, Snyder started again just before Thanksgiving in 1991 with a new flock of eighteen birds. Again, goshawks immediately started picking off any captive-raised parrots that refused to forage with the flock. In less than a month only eight remained. Although these birds had adjusted to the wild, a poor yield of pine nuts forced Noel Snyder to supplement their diet with food trays. When a goshawk took advantage of this convenient arrangement, he reluctantly recaptured the last four survivors. Further attempts at reintroducing thick-billed parrots to the Chiricahuas were unsuccessful, and Noel Snyder soon abandoned the effort.

Sometimes, no amount of dedication matters. Nature doesn't often allow us to correct our past mistakes. Still, there is a bit of hope for the parrots in Arizona. Recently, Helen Snyder wrote me, saying that thickbills are migrating along the Arizona–New Mexico border from the Mogollon Rim through the Animas Mountains. "The program has moved to Mexico," she said, "with a lot of work being done there on preserving the nesting areas close to the U.S. border."

Halfway up the chest-throbbing switchbacks my legs begin to ache. I take shorter steps, falling behind Chuck with his long, practiced strides. I notice we've left the oak-pine woodland behind. Douglas fir and ponderosa pine, both typical evergreens of the Madrean Montane Conifer Forest biotic community, lean into the slopes. Sunlight stabs through the conifers with deep incisions, igniting sheets of yellow needles at my feet and releasing a dry pine odor. It is the talcum smell of forest and dust, a smell that the trees hold close to the ground despite the occasional errant breeze. I pray for the wind, for the coolness passing over my sweat-rimmed skin. I pray for an end to the switchbacks, but the slope inclines to forty-five degrees and our trail continues slashing across it, back and forth, back and forth.

I hope for pairs of feathers.

Earlier, Chuck found two feathers on the trail. "One feather doesn't usually mean anything," he explained. "But two feathers together always means there's more." I rested while he began searching the ground, bits of down leading him like bread crumbs through the trees. Then he found the feather pile.

"What is it?" I asked, as Chuck picked through the yellow breast feathers and gray primaries.

"Probably a Grace's warbler killed by a sharp-shinned hawk."

Chuck has been *psshing* and squeaking periodically while we walk, and now, high on the switchbacks, he stops and begins whistling the low, monotonous "toots" of a northern pygmy owl.

Within moments, a single red-breasted nuthatch sounds off with a nasal *iink, iink, iink* in agitated repetition. Then another joins this one in dissonant chorus. While one dances and twitches, first right side up, next upside down, the other flies to within ten feet of my face. Chuck shifts to *psshing* and squeaking and other birds keep coming: tiny, half-ounce pine siskins, yellow-eyed juncos, yellow-rumped and black-throated gray warblers. Soon, the silhouettes of a dozen warblers flit high through the Douglas fir boughs. As the forest fills with trills and cheets and buzzes, I begin to laugh at the absurdity of it all. Who would have guessed that mimicking a little owl could set so many birds on edge?

After nearly three hours of hiking, spent mostly on some mean switchbacks, we achieve Morse Saddle. I drop my knapsack next to a fallen log and sit to peel an orange while a stiff wind chills my spine. A wooden signpost indicates that Monte Vista Lookout is another one and a half miles, and I know Chuck wants to try for it, but I'm spent. The peak's elevation is 9,357 feet, nearly another thousand-foot climb. For me, at least, the possibility of seeing short-tailed hawks there will have to come later.

As far as we know, no one has seen shorttails from Monte Vista Lookout, but that doesn't mean Chuck wouldn't find them there. Except for the one sighting at Paradise, the few records in the Chiricahuas all come from places around 8,000 feet: Rustler and Barfoot Parks, Barfoot Lookout (Buena Vista Peak), Barfoot Junction, Onion Saddle. Monte Vista Lookout meets the elevation criteria, although all the sightings are clustered six miles away to the north (where the roads bring the bird-watchers).

Short-tailed hawks hunt above these trees, "kiting" on the wind and swooping down among the branches in goshawk fashion to take small animals, mostly birds. The Chiricahuas seem to offer what shorttails need, which is a possible reason why the birds are coming to southeast Arizona. Appropriate habitat is the key. And, as John Arvin suggests, climate may also play an important role. Over the past ten thousand years, a warming and drying climate in the Southwest has driven more temperate species up mountain slopes into altitude pockets, leaving grasslands and deserts where forests and woodlands once stood. Only in the last one hundred years has the region seen the northward spread of mesquite trees, followed closely by the arrival of the collared peccary or javelina, an animal formerly limited to the tropics. Javelina bones are conspicuously absent from archaeological sites of southwestern Native Americans.

Plants and animals don't honor international boundaries or property lines. Species trespass by nature, responding to the flex and flux of climate and habitat over time. Even jaguars make occasional incursions into Arizona; in 1996 there were two, one in the nearby Peloncillo Mountains and another in the Baboquivari Mountains. Both animals were photographed and then left alone. Warner Glenn, the rancher who encountered the first borderland jaguar that year, and narrowly avoided a mauling thanks to his hounds, described the cat as having "fire in his eyes." When I look through the photographs he took, I see eyes with more than fire in them. I see eyes that look right though Warner Glenn and the circle of his dogs. These fiery eyes see through the human limitations of what we call wilderness.

It's after five when we get back to Sycamore Campground. I'm starved and sore, but not as sore as I anticipated for a six-mile mountainous hike. Chuck starts dinner—canned beef stew and Minute Rice—while I finish scrawling notes. The campground chipmunk has returned, a cliff chipmunk, the only kind that occurs in southern Arizona. The animal reminds me that more secretive animals like coatimundis and Mexican raccoons also visit the canyons of West Turkey Creek.

After sunset, we walk by flashlight to the Morse Canyon Trailhead, find a comfortable place to sit, and turn off our lights. The woodland envelops us; neither one of us speaks. We listen for whatever Turkey Creek offers us in the darkness. Stars leak through the trees, enough of them that I can pick out constellations. To the north, the Big Dipper spills its contents over Mormon Ridge. The wind has settled with the sun, and now, dry leaf-molds waft on the cool air. Somewhere down-canyon, a night bird calls with a clear rolling trill, the hollow, lonely plea of a whip-poor-will.

Grasses and water plants in Rucker Canyon

rucker canyon

Five-thirty A.M. Thirty-eight degrees Fahrenheit at creekside, Chuck reports. Rising from my sleeping bag takes willpower I'm not capable of mustering. Instead, I watch the sky lighten from plum to cerulean and listen to an introit of birdsong. This morning's choir service features the musical warble of a painted redstart as lead soprano.

After a breakfast of coffee and strawberries, Chuck and I hike up-canyon following the dry, boulder-strewn creek. Chuck, expecting action, wears his Zeiss binoculars around his neck and carries his Kowa spotting scope over one shoulder. I lug a black spiral notebook. Sycamore trees extend naked, white limbs above the oaks, and in one high arm, a pair of Arizona wood-peckers has excavated a nest, which they attend to regularly and noisily. The woodpeckers are another specialty here, a Mexican species whose range just extends into southeastern Arizona. Among grasses growing along the bank, we find a yellow-eyed junco nest with two gaping beaks nearly invisible within the bent and yellow stalks.

The first water we come to is a dark pool at the bottom of a grotto of gray rock, gray lichen, and yellow monkey flower. The water looks as thick and black as oil. White moth wings, clipped together in pairs, drift on the surface, flotsam for water striders to navigate. Mineral contour lines on the rocks mark the progress of evaporation as the liquid boundaries of the back swimmers and pineapple-smelling whirligig beetles implode upon them. The insects, however, have wings, and I imagine that even these may be expanding their ranges in search of more suitable habitats.

Riparian areas, those wildlife communities along the banks of rivers and streams, are corridors for these migrations of everything from the seeds of plants to the largest mammals. The corridors connect habitats as highways connect cities. Some riparian areas, such as the San Pedro River less than fifty miles from here, are important natural funnels for hundreds of species of animals migrating back and forth between the United States and Mexico. The San Pedro, a narrow ribbon of an oasis, claims over 82 different mammals and 380 birds, including gray hawks and yellow-billed cuckoos. In the Chiricahuas, high riparian canyons support galleries of sycamore, walnut, willow, and ash that spill into drier and warmer drainages dominated usually by cottonwood and willow, although others of the deciduous riparian appear there. These drainages connect biotic communities from the high montane conifer forests through oak-pine and encinal woodlands to the lower desert scrub and semidesert grasslands surrounding the mountains (including a four-hundred-mile umbilical to Mexico's Sinaloan thorn forest). Without these delicate green threads that trace the intermountain desert flats, ranges like the Chiricahuas would be cut off to most wildlife migration. The mountains really would be "sky islands."

Midmorning at our campsite, Chuck and I talk about our next move. We both agree that Barfoot Lookout at Buena Vista Peak should be our destination for seeing short-tailed hawks, but I favor the more leisurely route of driving through the less-traveled southern flanks of the Chiricahuas and visiting Rucker Canyon. From there, we can continue southeast through Tex Canyon and then northeast through the town of Apache, and approach the lookout from Portal, Arizona, and Cave Creek Canyon, the eastern gate to the mountains.

Rucker Canyon scoops out a three-thousand-foot gulch between broken and worn rhyolite cliffs in the southwestern corner of the Chiricahua Mountains. The canyon is named for Lieutenant John Anthony Rucker, an army officer who drowned in a flash flood here in the summer of 1878. The story has several versions but all agree that "Tony" Rucker was a dedicated officer and a hero. Born in Michigan, he entered West Point on July 1,

Summer grasses and mesquite trees in the southern Chiricahuas

1868, at the age of seventeen. In his sophomore year, however, the Academy discharged him after he failed mathematics and French. Evidently, Tony Rucker was able to gain his commission elsewhere, perhaps through the influence of his father, Major General Daniel H. Rucker (of Fort Rucker, Alabama, fame), and, in the summer of 1875, he joined the Sixth Cavalry in Arizona Territory. Once here, his orders included establishing a supply camp in this canyon and commanding a company of Apache scouts, duties for which he gained the admiration of his superiors. After Rucker's death, Captain William Carter of the Sixth Cavalry wrote in his report that "no officer in the army was better fitted for the work before him" and "who during his service with scouts followed nearly every hostile trail between the Gila River and the Sierra Madres in Mexico within a few hours after it was made."

Lieutenant Tony Rucker died trying to save the life of a fellow officer, Lieutenant Austin Henley, when Henley's horse stumbled while crossing a storm-swollen stream, tossing him into the torrent. Rucker dove in after him, but the river swept both men away. The officers were buried at Fort Bowie and later moved to the United States National Cemetery in San Francisco.

On April 29, 1879, Rucker's supply camp became Camp Rucker to honor the drowned lieutenant. Later called Fort Rucker, the outpost was important during the 1880s in the military's efforts to control the Chiricahua Apaches.

Rucker Canyon is the site of the infamous Apache battle called "The Campaign of the Rocky Mesa," which was the beginning of the end for Cochise, possibly the greatest of the Chiricahua Apache leaders. On October 5, 1869, Cochise and his band of warriors, camouflaged with weeds, attacked a west-bound mail coach near the Dragoon Mountains, thirty miles west of the Chiricahuas. They killed an escort of four soldiers, the driver, and Colonel John Finkle Stone, a thirty-three-year-old mine owner and popular citizen of Tucson. (Stone Avenue was later named for him.) The following day, in Sulphur Springs Valley, Cochise struck a group of cowboys herding cattle from Texas to California. The Apaches lanced to death one man and stole about two hundred head, but someone managed to escape and get word to Camp Bowie. Lieutenant William H. Winters and twenty-one cavalrymen immediately left in pursuit, the lieutenant learning of the stage attack en route. On October 8, Winters caught up with the Apaches, engaged them in a running skirmish, and recovered the cattle. Cochise and his band fled into what would later be known as Rucker Canyon.

When Captain Bernard, Winter's commander at Camp Bowie, arrived with sixty-one soldiers, he followed fresh tracks to a ridge above Red Rock and Rucker Canyons. It was a trap. The Apaches were waiting for them, holding their fire until the soldiers came within arrow shot. Two soldiers died in the fight, which continued until darkness when the Apaches slipped away.

Nearly a month of sporadic fighting between Cochise and the soldiers ensued. On November 2, after reinforcements joined Captain Bernard, soldiers swept through Rucker Canyon without finding any Apaches. Captain Bernard claimed victory (with an exaggerated death count of Apaches), having driven Cochise from the Chiricahua Mountains.

Although there would be other threats from Cochise, with raids on both sides of the border, the American and Mexican forces against him were relentless. He was growing old, his hair, tied with a yellow silk bandanna, showed streaks of silver. He had been at war nearly all of his life, the past nine years with U.S. soldiers, and he had grown tired. In the summer of 1870, he walked into Camp Mogollon and asked for peace.

Before he died five years later, Cochise helped establish a reservation for his people in their homeland, with the Chiricahua Mountains at its heart. The Chiricahua Reservation, covering more than three thousand square miles, excised a rectangle from southeast Arizona Territory, the Dragoon Mountains at the northwest corner. Unfortunately, the reservation wasn't popular with Territory citizens, even though peace with the Apaches had been successful in terms of the greatly reduced numbers of raids and killings. Less than two years after Cochise's death in the summer of 1875, the government dissolved the Chiricahua Reservation and ordered its residents relocated to the White Mountain agency, a hundred miles to the north. This wasn't the end of the Chiricahua Apache, however. Hundreds escaped into New Mexico Territory. About four hundred slipped away into the Sierra Madres, one of them a Bedonkohe Apache the Mexicans called Geronimo.

High in Rucker Canyon, water slips between gray boulders worn kneecap smooth and plunges into pools where oak leaves sail past tacking water striders. Monkey flower and top-heavy bunch grasses stitch the banks together in places, quickening the pulse of the creek. Fiery-eyed dragonflies rattle by on cellophane wings.

Stream in Rucker Canyon

Alongside the creek, a woodland of black walnut, Apache and Chihuahua pine, and oak drapes the canyon floor. Lichens, as dry and green as a dead man's goatee, fur the oaks' lowest branches, the growths diminishing as the trees move upslope. Here, Arizona cypress rise in high conical canopies, creating the largest stand of these evergreens in the Chiricahuas. I examine one cypress near the creek, a mature specimen of at least a hundred feet. The stringy, thinly furrowed bark twists counterclockwise in a slow spiral, completing a quarter turn every ten feet or so. I imagine the great tree pirouetting through the centuries as it grows.

At my feet, a lizard suddenly explodes through the cornflake leaves and sputters away leaving a smokeless trail. The reptiles are abundant in these wooded canyons. Of the species encountered so far, I've noted whiptails, their checkered flanks blurred by speed, and tail-flicking/taunting zebratails. The mountain spiny lizards always insist on banging out a few "push-ups," splitting sunlight with their scales into iridescent colors toward the violet end of the spectrum. Turquoise-shingled Clark spiny and eastern fence lizards are others I've seen among the twenty-five or so kinds found in these mountains.

Studies with lizards in the Chiricahuas suggest that the animals actually "see" their environment as whole patches of habitat rather than isolated rocks or fallen logs or tree trunks, and that the lizards don't select these patches randomly. What's important to these lizards is not a warm spot in the sun where mates and tasty insects pass by but an entire neighborhood of resources. The lizards understand the value of community. They show us that if we want to understand the ecology of any organism—from a paramecium to a porcupine—we must first consider the scale at which the organism perceives its world.

Perhaps this "perception" is what gives some species the ability to expand their ranges while others, particularly those a bit myopic like thick-billed parrots, have more difficulty. Researchers since 1993 have been studying Cooper's hawks nesting in Tucson's city parks, calling it a phenomenon. In 1995, when I first heard about it, I met with Clint Boal, a University of Arizona graduate student who was finishing his Ph.D. dissertation on urban Cooper's hawks. He had learned that the hawks had been nesting in Tucson for the previous five years and believed they had only recently arrived there. I wanted to know why.

Cooper's hawks seem most unlikely city dwellers. The hawks usually inhabit undeveloped woodlands like those of Turkey Creek and Rucker Canyon. Their short rounded wings and long narrow tails are adapted for quietly twisting and darting among tree branches and shrubs to chase down other birds, their primary prey. In this environment, the hawks are shy and secretive. In Tucson, however, Cooper's hawks hunt, court, and reproduce in a place where the human population exceeds half a million citizens. Researchers have counted as many as eighty active nests in one season, some of them densely packed—another urban behavioral shift—into neighborhoods and parks. In Tucson, families picnic on fried chicken under cottonwoods that spill feathers as hawks feast on doves.

Cooper's hawks aren't the only raptors invading Tucson,

but we know the most about these birds. We know that there are at least three likely reasons why the hawks nest in Tucson.

The first is trees. Large trees. Not the twisted resident mesquite or green-skinned paloverde but the huge, water-loving aliens like eucalyptus and aleppo pine, as well as our native cottonwood. The second reason is water. Cooper's hawks normally nest close to water, and the birds may be favoring the city's plethora of fountains, pools, birdbaths, and irrigation systems. But water in the desert also draws other birds, and this, along with the popularity of bird feeders, may account for the third and most important reason urban living agrees with Cooper's hawks: food.

Doves, both mourning and Inca, are some of Tucson's most common birds and are the hawks' primary prey. This abundance of food may actually permit the hawks to ignore what would otherwise be strict territorial boundaries, allowing them to nest much closer to each other, to adapt.

Could it be that the scale Cooper's hawks use to perceive their world is similar to the scale for other species? And that the scale is potentially unlimited? Even lizards see beyond their own pile of rocks. Could it be that humans are the most near-sighted creatures of all?

Rucker Canyon's frayed rhyolite scarps show red where huge wedges have slipped away in recent history and the slow moldering of lichens hasn't masked the natural color of the rock. Oaks everywhere are deciduous-dry, and gusts of wind loosen leaves that tumble to the ground with the sudden hard rataplan of a hail storm. Golden-brown layers carpet the landscape, softening the rock-cobbled hillsides. The canopy is a filigree against a hard, azurite sky, the shade skeletal. Tinder-brittle grasses smell like struck flint.

Farther down the canyon, Chuck and I unexpectedly flush a covey of Montezuma quail, the birds bursting from cover in pairs and triplets, pumping frenetic wings across the creek. Chuck is excited. He's been hoping to see the clown-faced ground bird in these mountains. Before this, we'd found only feathers—beautiful, white-spotted and fern-patterned shields suitable for headdresses.

We continue following the stream through a broad canyon wooded with sycamore, cypress, and pine. Pan-sized trout dart across the deepest pools, feral escapees from the now rubble-choked Rucker Lake where the Arizona Game and Fish Department once stocked the fish. (A sign at the lake reads: "Danger! Stay off lake bed. Possible quicksand.") At one pool, I watch a black-necked garter snake prowl the sandy bottom for fish or tadpoles until it ducks beneath a large submerged boulder.

"You haven't seen a fox squirrel yet, have you?" Chuck says, calling me over to a giant Apache pine.

I still don't see it. "Where?" I ask.

Chuck slowly circles the trunk of the tree, his face turned toward the high limbs. I look, but nothing appears. Then, when Chuck stands with the tree between us, the squirrel clambers into view, gripping the rough bark and peering directly at me. The squirrel is larger than I expected, longer-tailed than the rock and gray squirrels I'm familiar with in southern Arizona. And it's surprisingly red. Its fur shines like rusted metal against the dark pine bark.

The Mexican fox squirrel prefers the oak-pine woodlands, particularly in canyon bottoms with sycamore, ash, and walnut, but it may also reach higher elevations in Mexico. It ranges from extreme southeast Arizona south through the Sierra Madre Occidental and the western Mexican states of Nayarit (hence, the squirrel's scientific name, *Sciurus nayaritensis*) and Jalisco. In the Chiricahuas, scientists recognize one of the three subspecies of the Mexican fox squirrel. Called the Chiricahua fox squirrel, the plume-tailed, round-eared, ocher-flanked rodent inhabits only these mountains.

Chiricahua fox squirrels eat a varied diet, feeding largely on cypress nuts, acorns, juniper and pine seeds, walnuts, and mistletoe berries, and to a lesser degree on bark, leaves, flower buds, and a variety of fungi. This diverse diet most likely is a response to a drought-prone environment where trees may not produce seeds every year, providing a serious problem for animals with less cosmopolitan tastes. Thick-billed parrots might learn something from Chiricahua fox squirrels.

In the late afternoon, a pair of white-breasted nuthatches picks a meal from the bark of an Arizona cypress. The male, in a display of devotion, collects insects in his beak and then flies to his mate to offer her his selections, which she accepts. She must be eating for nine. She works the cypress for insects herself, spiraling up the trunk as if her beak were a phonograph needle in the grooves of the bark. I hear her quiet music, the burr of contentment.

Cave Creek

cave creek

With Chuck driving toward Apache, Arizona, across San Bernardino Valley, I watch flocks of Chihuahuan ravens spin and tumble in the wind over a blast of bone-white grassland that hurts my eyes. Kangaroo rat mounds swell above the grasses, the rodents' dark tunnels like eyes staring out of the loose red earth.

The town of Apache comprises little more than a few buildings, a trailer, and a schoolhouse, all gathered at roadside. One stone structure looks like it once may have been a country store and gas station that was later converted to a house, and is now deserted altogether.

"It was a post office, too," says my friend Mary Smith who lived on a ranch near Apache between 1938 and 1945 when she was a child. Mary's mother and father, who are buried in the Apache Cemetery, worked the ranch for seven years until her uncle, Jack Glass, inherited it at the age of seventeen. "We called it the Pitch Fork Ranch because of its brand, but its real name is Price Canyon Ranch and it's still a working guest ranch."

Mary went to grade school in Apache with the children of other ranchers and of the section workers who maintained a local and now defunct spur of the Southern Pacific Railroad. Needless to say, she had few classmates. One year, in second or third grade she thinks, she spent a whole year in school with only two other students, one of them her brother. "We got a lot of special attention," she says.

Now, on every Memorial Day weekend that she can, Mary returns to Apache. Next to the highway, a group of friends gathers in the corner of a cow pasture where parents and other loved ones rest. "We come to the cemetery every year for a cleanup and potluck, some of us from quite a ways."

Near the town, a sixteen-foot-high monument of cement-embedded stones and grinding metates commemorates the surrender of Geronimo a few miles from here on September 5, 1886. A plaque reads: "The surrender of Geronimo in Skeleton Canyon, on that historic day, forever ended Indian warfare in the United States." The city of Douglas erected the monument in 1934.

When Geronimo left the White Mountain Reservation for

the last time in May 1885 with 134 men, women, and children and crossed into Mexico's Sierra Madres, other Apache leaders like Juh, Chihuahua, and Naiche (the son of Cochise) joined him as well. It was this exodus that some Apaches would later say instigated their eventual relocation to Florida and imprisonment. They had reason to believe this. Four months after the departure, 20 warriors crossed back into Arizona and started raiding and killing ranchers and prospectors in the Chiricahuas, eluding soldiers for months and angering citizens of Tucson. Then, beginning in November of 1885, Apaches swept through the New Mexico and Arizona territories, attacking miners, ranchers, and freight wagons, while frustrating cavalry pursuers for months. When the Apaches returned to their Sierra Madres refuge, after traveling twelve hundred miles, stealing 250 horses, and killing an estimated 38 people, they had lost only one man.

Brigadier General George Crook, a quiet, taciturn officer who believed that only Apaches could track down and locate Apaches, enlisted Apache scouts. With Lieutenant Charles B. Gatewood in command, they set out to find and arrange a meeting with Geronimo. During discussions with Crook on March 25 and 27 of 1886, Geronimo, Naiche, and Chihuahua agreed to surrender, provided that after two years in prison they might return to the reservation. Crook accepted the provision. But later, after hearing that they would be tried and hanged instead, Geronimo and Naiche with 37 men, women, and children bolted in a rainstorm. On April 2, a telegram from President Cleveland said he would not honor the conditions of the surrender. The Apaches Geronimo left behind were loaded onto a train and never returned to Arizona. General Crook resigned from his command.

On April 12, 1886, Brigadier General Nelson A. Miles assumed command of Fort Bowie, certain that regular soldiers without Apache scouts could subdue Geronimo. Geronimo easily eluded them, while continuing to raid and kill settlers and soldiers without losing any of his own men. By the following summer, General Miles was using Apache scouts and ordering Gatewood back into Mexico. It was two of Gatewood's scouts who convinced Geronimo to talk with the lieutenant, whereupon Gatewood made it clear to the Apache leader that his only option upon surrender was imprisonment. Gatewood didn't know that President Cleveland had told General Miles to take Geronimo prisoner only if he could not hang him, which Cleveland "much prefer[red]." Learning that Chihuahua and the other Apaches he had left behind the previous spring were already in Florida, Geronimo, visibly shaken, agreed to meet General Miles at Skeleton Canyon.

On September 5, General Nelson Miles took personal custody of Geronimo and Naiche. Within a few days all of the remaining Chiricahua Apaches—those who were peaceful at the White Mountain Reservation, the renegade warriors and their followers, and even the Apache scouts responsible for Geronimo's capture—boarded trains headed for Florida. The region was finally free for settlement (or resettlement). Only rumors, and the occasional appearance of moccasined footprints, would continue to inspire people's fears of the Apache.

We continue on to the town of Portal, Arizona, at the mouth of Cave Creek Canyon. From the store and café, Chuck and I walk up Rock House Road to Dave Utterback's place ("Walkers Welcome"). Portal, at 4,775 feet, lies in the Upper Sonoran life zone, or more specifically the Semidesert Grassland biotic community, where the fruiting stalks of century plants, soaptree yucca, and desert spoon picket grassy hillsides among clumps of prickly pear cacti. Mesquite trees, unfurling fuzzy, yellow catkins, catclaw mimosa, and gray-stemmed hackberry trees file down the drainages and wide valleys.

Like other residences in Portal, Dave Utterback's home is a construction of smooth river stones. Blooming pomegranate shrubs lean against the walls on both sides of the door, which is open to visitors. In the enclosed porch, tables display plastic-sleeved reprints of Dave's wildlife pencil drawings for sale. I thumb through all the boxes of cards and posters, impressed with the fine detail and realism of his art. Gray fox, great horned and barred owls, red-tailed and rough-legged hawks—the fur and feathers are exquisite and look so soft that I touch them expecting to feel their texture beneath my fingers. I buy packages of cards, leaving money in a self-pay box.

We follow a path to an adjacent building where a wooden plank set on concrete blocks faces a sycamore grove. Two people sit on the bench, and we join them. The place swarms with hummingbirds, and we instantly identify several rosy-bibbed male broadtails by the metallic whir of their slotted wings. The bluethroats and violet-crested magnificents fan their tails and dwarf all others, driving off the broadbills and blackchins and

Century plants near Sulphur Canyon

Anna's, which zip around a half acre of feeding stations made up of a dozen sugar-water bottles swinging from tree branches, wires, and the dried, branching stalk of a century plant. Sections of citrus fruit draw orange- and grapefruit-colored warblers and orioles, while pine siskins, lesser goldfinches, and bridled titmice prefer the seed-feeders.

Two tree lizards scuttle over a pile of weathered boards, the blue-bellied, orange-throated male chasing a disinterested female. Then the lizards abandon the woodpile to a cliff chipmunk that stutters up to a dripping pan of water for a drink. The chipmunk amuses the couple next to us with its comic behavior, stretching out on its belly and waving its tail in serpentine mimicry.

The woman wears a straw pith helmet over fine gray hair, a small compass mounted on the hat's brim. Her husband, in white beard and glasses, peers through binoculars under his ball cap. Both raise binoculars to their faces with each new bird entrance. The woman is quicker and more accurate with the identifications.

When another couple arrives with a German friend, Chuck introduces me to Bob and Janet Witzeman, who I soon learn are Phoenix celebrities of the Arizona birding community. Chuck and the Witzemans launch into a discussion that I can't quite penetrate although I hear words like, "Flame-colored tanager fifteen minutes above mine shaft Miller Canyon." (Are these coordinates or directions?) Or several variations of, "We're going for . . ." followed by assorted names and numbers: "Charley's 486" and "Bix's 490." When Chuck sees my confusion, he explains that Charley and Bix are the lead runners in the state for the number of bird species sighted in Arizona by one person. "Isn't this great?" he says. "You always meet the same people. It's like we're all Deadheads."

I laugh at his analogy that avid bird-watchers compare to the devoted fans/groupies of the Grateful Dead band. It seems appropriate.

A man in khaki shorts and a worn T-shirt arrives carrying a plastic wastebasket. "Any of you throw away a lizard?" he asks, setting it down so we can look inside.

"Hi, Dave," several people reply in unison, and I realize that he is Dave Utterback. He's younger than I imagined, late forties maybe, his black hair flecked with gray. The lizard is a Clark's spiny, which dropped into Dave's wastepaper basket and couldn't escape. Dave thought to share it with us before releasing it to his woodpile.

More birding conversation ensues. Dave asks us to record any female broad-billed hummingbirds, which he's expecting will migrate through soon.

"Have you seen a Lucifer?" Chuck asks, wanting to add the species to his state life list.

"Two weeks ago," he says, "but none recently. You might try the Spoffords' place."

When Janet mentions the recent sighting of a snow bunting in Arizona near the town of Thatcher, only the second ever recorded in the state (the first was in 1981), everyone has personal birding stories to relate and the discussion begins rising to crescendo. And, as if the birds weren't a sufficient topic, Dave tells us about a very large bear that broke into his house and raided his kitchen the previous night. "He had no problem getting to my feeders, either," he says, stretching his arms above his lanky frame toward the hanging bottles, which remain out of reach.

Taking seriously Dave's tip about the Lucifer hummingbird, Chuck drives about a mile farther up the canyon, and we park with several other vehicles near a ranch house. A sign on the gate welcomes us to the feeders (7:30 A.M. to 5:30 P.M.). At the end of a short path leading to the backyard of the home, nine people sit in an amphitheater of rough benches and chairs, facing a string of bird feeders of various kinds, including suet traps and thistle bags. A man named Hugh quietly introduces himself to an older woman with white hair cropped short, wearing a flower print dress, who seems to be the center of attention. "We've been coming here for twelve years," he says to Sally Spofford. "We love your place, and it's so good to finally meet you."

Chuck speaks with Sally for a few minutes about a mutual acquaintance and then finds a seat at the far end of the group. I stand behind Sally, listening.

"I seem to have a resident coral snake," she says to a man sitting next to her.

"And you're not afraid?"

"Oh, they're so beautiful. I've held them in my hand."

Sally Spofford, a Cornell University ornithologist who retired here with her husband Walter in 1972, is affectionately called "The Bird Lady of Portal." Her home, the Aquila Rancho (Eagle Ranch) but better known as "Spoffords," is famous for hummingbirds, and people come from all over the world to sit in Sally's backyard and watch her feeders. It is the most reliable place to see Lucifer hummingbirds in Arizona, and the "yard list" reportedly rivals any other in the United States with not only rare hummingbirds but other uncommon species like fox and golden-crowned sparrows. Fortunate bird-watchers might even see an Aztec thrush or a brilliant, blue mockingbird. Chuck would settle for a Lucifer, but this day none is forthcoming.

Our next stop, Steward Campground, at about 5,000 feet, is still in the Upper Sonoran life zone. But now, instead of the Semidesert Grassland, a Madrean Evergreen Woodland biotic community dominates the landscape with resident oaks, pine, and tessera-barked juniper. The campground huddles in a riparian corridor of sycamore, walnut, and other thirsty trees.

We head for campsite number two, past a travel trailer parked next to a picnic table bedecked with vases of flowers and lighting equipment. A magnificent hummingbird visits several blooms but the photographer is nowhere in sight.

Sally Spofford had been talking about Steward Campground's site number two, and how hundreds of bird-watchers were angered after the Forest Service began cutting "hazardous" branches from trees along roads and in campgrounds. Unwittingly, the crews had removed a sycamore limb with a cavity where a whiskered screech owl had nested every year. "Many people saw their first whiskered in this place," Chuck tells me as we pull into the campsite. "Famous number two. Helen Snyder brought me here. I'll show you."

I don't see my first whiskered screech owl—or any owl for that matter. Instead, high in the tree, I see a dark oval scar where someone attempting to correct a mistake has fastened a severed limb with an empty cavity.

Steward Campground lies half a mile downstream from the most popular bird-watching location in the Chiricahuas, and quite possibly in the state: South Fork Cave Creek. The defile hosts a variety of habitats, from the deciduous sycamore-ash riparian drainage to woodlands of oak and cypress to forests of pine and fir. It's this mix of biotic communities that draws both tropical and temperate species, some of them very rare. South Fork lists seventy-four species of mammals, thirty-one snakes, twenty-four lizards, and twelve amphibians. White-tailed deer forage with javelina and black bears with coatimundis. Years ago, jaguars may have stalked deer in this canyon. And every so often, someone sees a jaguarundi, the long-bodied, charcoal-colored cat of Mexican woodlands.

But mostly, it's the birds that bring the visitors. South Fork lays claim to the first flame-colored tanager *and* the first eared trogon recorded in the United States. The canyon is probably also the most convenient place in the country to see that much-sought "life bird" of bird-watchers, the elegant trogon, first spotted here in 1942. In fact, of the fifty thousand plus people that visit southeast Arizona every year looking for birds, as many as half of them come to South Fork to see this iridescent, emerald and geranium-feathered, parrot-like bird.

The ornithologist W.E.D. Scott published the first record

Sycamore trees

of elegant trogons north of Mexico based on an eyewitness description from the Santa Catalina Mountains in the fall of 1884, but the sighting was unconfirmed. Then, on August 24, 1885, an off-duty army officer from Fort Huachuca named Lieutenant H.C. Benson killed one of the birds in the Huachuca Mountains. Fifty-four years later, in 1939, Cornell University ornithologist Dr. Arthur Allen found the first nest north of the border in the Santa Rita Mountains. Because it's unlikely that ornithologists before the 1880s would have missed the conspicuous bird, some experts currently believe that trogons only recently have been colonizing the few mountain ranges in southeast Arizona, pushing their ranges northward for at least the last century. Although their number have decreased lately due to drought, from the 1980s to mid-90s an estimated fifty pairs were migrating north into the United States each spring to nest. And some of these have stayed. According to Rick Taylor, in 2001–02, "no fewer that six different trogons were known to over-winter, which is probably a record." I've seen them from the Peloncillos at our border with New Mexico, west to Madera Canyon in the Santa Ritas. But it's in South Fork Cave Creek that the greatest number of elegant trogons nests in this country.

Rick Taylor knows trogons. It was Rick Taylor who, in 1977, sighted the first eared trogon—a close relative of the elegant trogon—in the United States. In 1979, *Audubon Magazine* dubbed him "Arizona's resident trogon expert." His book, *Trogons of the Arizona Borderlands,* is the seminal volume on trogons.

"Elegant Trogons often seem to arrive in border ranges already paired," Taylor writes in his book, the birds showing up in the Chiricahuas not as a wave but sporadically on "almost any still, moonlit night in April." Trogons favor riparian canyons that bisect oak-pine woodlands where they most often nest in natural or woodpecker-chiseled, flicker-enlarged cavities in sycamore trees. Female trogons, which are less colorful than males but still striking with their brown plumage and large eyes, share with their mates the incubation and feeding duties, feeding the young on fruits and insects even after they leave the nest. Trogons usually nest once in a season in Arizona but may return to the same cavity for several years.

The song of the elegant trogon is both singular and haunting, a sound one might expect to hear where spiders unfurl web-hammocks over tannin-stained grottos and trees screen sunlight through a thousand apertures. I always hear trogons before I see them. The usual song is described variously as similar to a hen turkey, a frog, or tearing cardboard. It pulses through the woodland normally during the few hours following dawn in April or May when males voice territories and courtship intentions. Perched upright on a branch, he drops his tail and throws back his head, emitting a deep, throaty *ko-ah, ko-ah, ko-ah, ko-ah, ko-ah, ko-ah*. It's unforgettable.

The Southwestern Research Station, at 5,400 feet, is our next stop, as Chuck and I continue the climb through Cave Creek Canyon. The station, a facility of the American Museum of Natural History, sits next to a grove of cottonwood and sycamore trees near the confluence of North Fork and Cave Creek.

Researchers from all over the world, as well as others interested in the Chiricahuas, live in the station's cabins and eat meals in a common dining room.

Steven Bayden Reed originally settled the property in 1878—79, where he and his father built a cabin (and a wagon road to the cabin) and called the place the Steven B. Reed Ranch. Reed's family was the first to settle in the Chiricahua Mountains. Over the years the property transferred to others, becoming the Bide-a-wee Ranch in 1921 and then the Painted Canyon Ranch in 1946, when the owners operated it as a dude ranch. In 1950, Weldon and Phyllis Heald bought the ranch, and lived there for five years before selling it to the American Museum of Natural History in 1955. (Weldon Heald, a naturalist and author of the wonderful book *Sky Island,* published in 1967 and again in 1975 under the new title, *The Chiricahua Mountains,* originally coined the term "sky island" to describe his home.) Since then, the Southwestern Research Station has added acreage and additional facilities, including housing units, a swimming pool, and a volleyball court. Its Osborn Memorial Laboratory holds a library, insect and vertebrate collections, a herbarium, and a photography lab. There are also other technical equipment research labs, outdoor aviaries, and an Animal Behavior Observatory available for scientists.

In the late 1980s and early 1990s, Noel Snyder centered his thick-billed parrot reintroduction program at the station. Recent research has involved several long-term studies on predator avoidance in horned lizards, social behavior and communication in kangaroo rats, the behavioral ecology of yellow-eyed juncos, communal breeding in Mexican jays, the social behaviors of ants, and, my favorite, the "flywheel" evolution of parthenogenetic lizards.

Parthenogenetic lizards reproduce without sex, a behavior unknown among vertebrate animals until 1958 when the Soviet herpetologist Ilya Darevsky first noted it. After collecting lizards in Armenia and learning that every specimen in his collection was female, Darevsky boldly announced that certain species of lizards have only one gender. He was right. Soon after Darevsky published his research, another herpetologist, Richard Zweifel, found a unisexual species of whiptail lizard in the Chiricahuas. The lizards are all females, and they reproduce in the absence of males by laying eggs that hatch into clones.

As they have been doing for three decades, husband and wife herpetologists Jay Cole and Carol Townsend still carry on the research Richard Zweifel started at the Southwestern Research Station. "We have been working on such things as whether the absence of males is real; how many species are like this and where do they exist; how do they reproduce; what are their patterns of inheritance; how did they originate," Jay told me recently. The couple collects whiptail females here and carts them back to a lab at the American Museum of Natural History in New York City, where the lizards bask under ultraviolet lights in sandy-bottomed terrariums, laying eggs that no male has fertilized. And the eggs hatch. Jay and Carol have raised seven generations of lizards in this way, the first parthenogenetic lizards ever raised in captivity.

It seems that all-female whiptail lizards arose rapidly in response to disturbed or fluctuating habitats (such as the desertification of grassland in the Southwest), where different whiptail species came in contact, interbred, and produced hybrid offspring. Although all the males were sterile and would die out in one generation, the females could lay eggs with a full complement of chromosomes rather than the normal half. Perfect clones of the mother resulted. Today, scientists recognize more than a dozen species of unisexual whiptails; they are, essentially, animal "weeds," capable of taking advantage of new territory by moving in and quickly populating it. The lizards don't just "see" past the limitations of their environment, they see right through the restrictions of gender.

In the late afternoon we drive over 7,600-foot Onion Saddle, and turn south to climb toward Barfoot Junction. Chuck thinks we should camp tonight among the open ponderosa pine and Douglas fir of the junction and hike to Barfoot Lookout before dawn tomorrow. "Just seeing the sunrise will be worth it," he says, "and it's the best place for shorttails." The lookout is where Chuck saw the hawk last August.

From the Southwestern Research Station to the crossing at East Turkey Creek, our route has taken us out of the Madrean Evergreen Woodland and into the Madrean Montane Conifer Forest biotic community of largely pine and fir, with silverleaf and lobe-leafed Gambel oak. At Onion Saddle we find white pine, a common evergreen of high elevations and moist, rocky slopes.

We pass Barfoot Junction without stopping, only slowing

down enough to see that our campsite is unoccupied, and continue to Barfoot Park through a dense and well-developed mixed conifer forest of Douglas fir, white fir, and white pine. Chuck stops near a cattle guard. "This is the place where Rick Taylor had the shorttails," he says, and we get out to look around.

The air is cool and breezy. The hyperbolic smell of pine, together with the prospect of actually encountering such a rare bird in the Chiricahuas, begins to charge my emotions. I start to believe it could happen.

At Barfoot Park we meet Larry, the only person in the campground, and he claims to have seen the hawks earlier this afternoon. The news excites us. Larry sits in a camp chair next to his red Ford Ranger, a sleeping bag unrolled in the truck's bed. He wears a denim jacket and purple Miami Dolphins cap, his windburned face turned toward the meadow under Buena Vista Peak. He's waiting for a visit from several black bears, which he's baited with an open can of tuna. "It'll get busy here in a few minutes," he says in a wonderful Texas accent.

Chuck unpacks his spotting scope and heads across the meadow, muttering something about habituated bears and death sentences. Buena Vista Peak juts up directly east, a naked dome of rhyolite, skirted with conifers and then aspen higher on the talus slopes. Barfoot Lookout, with its yellow walls and five dark windows, caps the apex of the peak at 8,823 feet above sea level.

Talus slopes are important here. To the north, another field of broken rock inclines to the crumbling cliffs and jagged spires of Barfoot Peak. These rough slopes are home to twin-spotted rattlesnakes, one of three shy, diminutive rattlesnakes found only in the high mountain ranges in southeastern Arizona and northern Mexico. But even ridge-nosed and rock rattlesnakes, the other two small-bodied species, don't range this high. Twinspots even live above 10,000 feet, altitudes greater than any other rattlesnake in Arizona.

Twin-spotted rattlesnakes are pit vipers that rarely exceed two feet in length, and that may be active throughout the year, even at the highest elevations. They accomplish this by choosing warm places to bask in the sun. Most activity, however, takes place after the monsoons arrive in July, when the reptiles begin hunting lizards, an unusual primary food for rattlesnakes. Mating occurs in August and September, with females apparently storing sperm during the winter and then giving birth to live young the next summer in July or August.

The greatest threat to twin-spotted rattlesnakes comes as a result of their uniqueness and rarity. These characteristics make the reptiles valuable to collectors. Studies conducted with twinspots at Barfoot Park show that, as a result of collecting pressure from pet traders, the snakes are smaller than those found at nearby unhunted sites. Unfortunately, Barfoot Park is renowned as a twin-spotted rattlesnake haven, something as deadly for the snakes as opened cans of tuna are for the bears.

After dinner, Chuck and I decide to walk in the dark from our campsite at Barfoot Junction down the road to Rustler Park. Tomorrow will be our last day in the Chiricahuas and our best opportunity to see short-tailed hawks, or possibly even locate a nest. But tonight, under a moonless sky clouded with stars, we talk not so much about finding things outside as revealing things inside. Nature affects us this way, it seems. We cannot enter nature without nature penetrating us.

In the roadside cuts, glow worms send messages at the speed of light. Cool, blue-green, bioluminescent photons shine in the darkness, carrying the intentions of insect nerve ganglia to neighboring glow worms, to our eyes, and to the very stars themselves. I wonder, is it only the glow worms that can interpret the intentions?

My friend, the nature writer and poet Alison Deming, says that the human soul comprehends no boundary, no edge. We draw lines on maps, erect fences and walls, designate what's wilderness and what's not, but it means nothing. Life trespasses. Even my skin is permeable. At times when the air is still and warm, I can't feel where my skin ends and the world begins. Individuality is a myth. We are all connected to one another, not in delineated and arranged life "zones" but in a fluid mosaic of life communities where rattlesnakes sun themselves among pines and bears, and insects might communicate with stars.

Cochise Head and the Heart of Rocks,
Chiricahua National Monument

barfoot lookout

With the incandescence of molten lava, the rising sun ignites San Simon Valley. Standing on Buena Vista Peak at Barfoot Lookout, on the rim of an ancient caldera, I'm looking east twenty-seven million years into the past, when this whole region shook with wild volcanic eruptions. To the west, the shadow of the Chiricahuas pushes across Sulphur Springs Valley and rises into a reef of clouds like a fault block mountain thrusting up from the earth's crust. In this way, dawn graces me with a hint of what the land remembers of its beginnings in this place.

The wind cuts through my jacket and sweatshirt making

the forty-six degrees Fahrenheit temperature feel closer to the negative side of the scale. At four this morning, Chuck and I fought the wind and chill to leave our sleeping bags and climb five hundred feet in the darkness to the lookout. Chuck, whose Flagstaff lungs and red blood cells savor this high, thin air, quickly outpaced me, even carrying his camp chair and ever-present spotting scope. I struggled up the steep mile with knapsack, chair, and coffee cup but still gained the summit shortly after five and before the sunrise.

Now, with cold-stiffened and cracked hands, I write notes while slowly turning 360 degrees. In the north, Cochise Head, a mile-long rock formation and perfect hawk-nosed profile of the Apache chief, faces the sky. To the east, sunlight bleeds through long fingers of clouds lying low among corrugations of mountains, seven . . . no, eight ragged and torn ridges in succession all the way to the horizon. To the south, Fly Peak at 9,666 feet, is the second highest peak in the range after 9,796-foot Chiricahua Peak a few miles farther south along the knobby backbone of the mountains. A subalpine conifer forest of fir and spruce girdles Fly Peak. The Engelmann spruce on the north- and east-facing slopes of Chiricahua Peak represent the famous southernmost stand of the trees on the continent. And finally, in the west, the yellow and umber patchwork of Sulphur Springs Valley reaches toward the twin peaks of the Huachuca Mountains. From this vantage point, I can even see as far as the blue-gray dimple of Mount Wrightson in the Santa Rita Mountains, 150 miles away.

Birds sing below us on the forested slopes and Chuck checks

them off like he's taking classroom attendance: yellow-eyed junco, hairy woodpecker, hermit thrush, yellow-rumped warbler, warbling vireo, western bluebird, Virginia's warbler, red-breasted nuthatch. I can't see a single one, only the white-throated swifts leaning paddlelike wings into the sky.

At seven-thirty, Chuck has a possible short-tailed hawk in the distance. "He seems stocky, short-tailed," he says, one eye at his spotting scope. "But then all the buteos are short-tailed." He follows the hawk with his scope across the sky to a ridgeline about two miles away where it perches on a dead, burned-out snag. "Maybe a redtail, but no red flash in the sunlight." Then the hawk flies over the ridge and disappears.

"Well, things are happening," Chuck says optimistically. "The birds are up."

Buteo is the classification given to the group of hawks with broad wings and round tails, the "soaring" hawks that people usually see turning lazy circles over desert flats or stationed on a roadside power pole. Red-tailed hawks are the most common. Other buteos include the prairie-hugging Swainson's hawk; shy, woodland hawks like the red-shouldered and broad-winged; and the zone-tailed hawk, a buteo of riparian canyons. Short-tailed hawks look like broadwings with longer, more rounded wings. Two color variations or "morphs" exist: a light morph and a dark, with dark being predominant in the population. The difference between the two morphs is so great—an entirely white-breasted bird versus an entirely black bird—that the two hawks appear like separate species.

Observers have reported light morphs in the Chiricahuas,

as well as juvenile birds, according to a species account compiled by Michael G. Shepard. He reports, "It is clear that there are at least two light morph birds, one of them an adult and the other a juvenile . . . a juvenile was seen several times from Barfoot Park . . . it was observed soaring, and it perched briefly in a bare tree on Barfoot Peak. On the 23rd, a bird of unknown age seen from Barfoot Lookout (atop Buena Vista Peak) at 2 P.M. pursued and caught a small bird." The short-tailed hawk Chuck saw here last year was a light morph, an adult chasing a red-tailed hawk. He also thought he could hear a juvenile hawk calling from the trees, one reason he believes the hawks may be nesting in the Chiricahuas.

At nine it's warmer, with a strong breeze out of the west. We haven't seen much hawk activity of any kind, only ravens and a few "zone-tailed vultures," as Chuck calls them, unable to distinguish between the turkey vultures and their impostors at this distance. (Zone-tailed hawks mimic vultures as a hunting strategy.) Chuck concentrates on the southern crest, while I watch over the north. I look for shadows undulating across the terrain and for the birds joined to them but nothing presents itself and so my eyes stray to other interests. One of these is a many-fingered drainage where a flat section of the mountains drops away into canyons of silent stone hoodoos—the twelve-thousand-acre Chiricahua National Monument.

Botanist Janice Emily Bowers writes that, "Chiricahua National Monument is, more than anything else, a monument to erosion." This is most apparent from where I sit, above and somewhat removed from the overwhelming crowds of stone. I can see how, if it weren't for some long past potent work of water and gravity, the monument would be nothing more than a mesa, a tableland spread with a thin cloth of green. Instead, erosion has exposed a buried history, splitting open huge layered blocks of welded and unwelded tuff, which water and ice have gradually shaped according to the whim of rock and time. Erosion has quarried this medium and, with hands like Michelangelo, has chiseled and smoothed and polished it to free the art hidden within.

Twelve thousand acres is relatively small when compared to the entire Chiricahua range, hardly enough space to hide in—unless you turn the area into a maze of hoodoo-dominated canyons. The place is as convoluted as a human brain but on a massive scale; you could lose a troop of soldiers in there, or perhaps a band of reclusive Apaches. There are a few stories: In 1890, nearly four years after Geronimo's surrender at Skeleton Canyon, a homesteader named Hugh Stafford found the fresh track of a large moccasin near his cabin in Bonita Canyon, at the mouth of what is now the monument. One of Stafford's horses was missing. Nearby, he noticed another, smaller footprint, possibly a woman's. After an incident in Pinery Canyon involving a ransacked cabin and moccasin tracks, soldiers from Fort Bowie followed the tracks to a rocky outcrop at the top of Rhyolite Canyon. There the trail turned cold. Today, the place is called Massai Point, after "Bigfoot" Massai, a Chiricahua Apache who once served as an army scout and escaped the reservation fate of his people. Somewhere near St. Louis, Massai jumped from the

Organ pipe formation, Chiricahua National Monument

prison train bound for Florida. Many believe that the footprints Stafford and the soldiers found were Massai's and those of a Mescalero Apache woman he had kidnapped, but no one ever saw evidence of them again. I like to think that their descendants might still roam these canyons.

Roughly twice the size of Chiricahua National Monument, the Chiricahua Wilderness Area lays its borders around the highest peaks at the heart of the mountains. The place is a roadless, forested, high country preserve between the 6,100-foot canyon bottom of South Fork Cave Creek and 9,796-foot Chiricahua Peak. The wilderness area protects not only the southernmost stand of Engelmann spruce in North America, but such rare and interesting species as twin-spotted rattlesnakes and Mexican chickadees, the latter whose range just barely creeps into southeast Arizona and southwest New Mexico. In fact, this mixed Chiricahua community of pine-fir and fir-spruce forests is the only place north of Mexico where Mexican chickadees breed.

I can see part of the wilderness area to the south off Chuck's left shoulder. Knowing it's there makes me wonder about our need for wilderness areas, for our need to restrict and set aside nature. For what? Itself? For our own peace of mind? Shouldn't we protect all life regardless of placement? Establishing wilderness areas is a kind of taming. We hope the wildlife is content within the plot of ground, that it remains there in safety and doesn't venture beyond those borders to interfere with us, with our day-to-day civilized activities of growth and prosperity. It's

a strange irony, I think, these reservations we create for the sub-
jugated. Why are there none for others who once ranged in these
mountains? For the wolf and the jaguar and the grizzly bear?
For the Chiricahua Apache?

At 10 A.M., Chuck and I begin packing up our gear and prepar-
ing to descend Barfoot Lookout and the Chiricahua Mountains.
It's time to return home. We're a bit disappointed by not finding
any short-tailed hawks, but our search for them has been far
from fruitless, and the hawks will undoubtedly be in these mountains when we return. For me, simply looking for them has been
rewarding. My notebook shows 102 different species of birds
for the trip, many of them new to me. But more than experienc-
ing all these birds, and this wild place they inhabit, I've encountered a new perception of my world, an expanding perception,
perhaps even one of wilderness defined as wildlife sees it. I may
have to come to the Chiricahuas to see fox squirrels and trogons
and short-tailed hawks because for now this is their home. But
I don't have to come here to see wilderness. I don't have to
travel at all. Nature always pushes the limits, blurs the lines.
Birds violate our airspace. Weeds encroach upon our sidewalks
and streets. Insects invade our homes. We are part of it. Wilderness is not only a place "over there," something we place on a
map. Wilderness is the privet hedges and thistles and dung-hunt-
ing beetles in our own backyards.

Halfway down the trail, a mixed flock of juncos and warblers
and nuthatches scatters through the pines like dry leaves untreed

by a gust of wind. Among these birds, Chuck points out to me, are a few Mexican chickadees, their distinctive nasal trill penetrating all neighboring bird voices. My first Mexican chickadees: I add them to my notebook with an asterisk—species number 103. Like so many others I've seen and thought about over the last four days, this one also speaks to me. At the turn of the last century, art historian and southwestern sojourner John Van Dyke wrote: "Nature does not bend the elements to favor the plants and animals; she makes the plants and animals do the bending." Cranes stepping over winter cornfields. Lizards crossing sexual barriers. Snow-country parrots and rattlesnakes. Hypothetical short-tailed hawks. My own expanding ecological awareness. And now this tiny, almost insignificant bird rides the frontlines of an invasion from the south, subtly fighting for place, bending, adapting, and, like the Chiricahua Mountains themselves, bridging the borders of wildness.

bibliography

Bennett, Peter S., R. Roy Johnson and Michael R. Kunzmann. *An Annotated Checklist of Vascular Plants of the Chiricahua Mountains*. Special Report No. 12. United States Geological Survey, Biological Resources Division. University of Arizona, 1996.

Berry, Wendell. *What Are People for? Essays by Wendell Berry*. New York: North Point Press, 1990.

Best, Troy L. "Sciurus nayaritensis," *Mammalian Species*, no. 492 (Jun 1995): 1.

Bowers, Janice Emily. *Chiricahua National Monument*. Tucson: Southwest Parks and Monuments Association, 1988.

Brown, David E. *Borderland Jaguars.* Salt Lake City: University of Utah Press, 2001.

————., ed. *Biotic Communities: Southwestern United States and Mexico*. Salt Lake City: University of Utah Press, 1994.

———., ed. *The Wolf in the Southwest: The Making of an Endangered Species.* Tucson: University of Arizona Press, 1983.

Chronic, Halka. *Roadside Geology of Arizona.* Missoula: Mountain Press Publishing, 1983.

Cockrum, Lendell E. *Mammals of the Southwest.* Tucson: University of Arizona, 1982.

Glenn, Warner and Ray Turner. *Eyes of Fire: Encounter with a Borderlands Jaguar.* El Paso: Printing Corner Press, 1996.

Hayes, Alden. *A Portal to Paradise.* Tucson: University of Arizona Press, 1999.

Heald, Weldon F. *The Chiricahua Mountains.* Tucson: University of Arizona Press, 1967.

Kleese, William C. "Military Posts of Territorial Arizona: Fort Rucker." *Copper State Journal,* vol. 32, no. 4 (Winter 1997): 135.

Koprowski, John L. and Michael C. Corse. "Food Habits of the Chiricahua Fox Squirrel *(Sciurus nayaritensis chiricahuae),*" *The Southwestern Naturalist,* no. 46 (Mar 2001): 62.

Kunzmann, Michael R., et al. "Elegant Trogon," *The Birds of North America,* no. 357 (1998): 1.

Lamberton, Ken. "Thick-billed Parrots," *Bird Watcher's Digest* (Nov/Dec 1993): 48.

Lowe, Charles H. *Arizona's Natural Environment: Landscapes and Habitats.* Tucson: University of Arizona, 1964.

Monson, Gale and Allan R. Phillips. *Annotated Checklist of the Birds of Arizona,* 2nd edition. Tucson: University of Arizona Press, 1981.

Negri, Sam. "Chiricahua Memories," *Tucson Weekly* (Dec 10–16, 1998): 2.

Phillips, Steven J. and Patricia Wentworth Comus, eds. *A Natural History of the Sonoran Desert.* Tucson: Arizona-Sonora Desert Museum Press, 2000.

Prival, David B., et al. *A Comparative Study of Hunted vs. Unhunted Populations of the Twin-Spotted Rattlesnake.* Final Report. Wildlife and Fisheries Science, School of Renewable Natural Resources. University of Arizona, 1999.

Quammen, David. *The Song of the Dodo: Island Biogeography in an Age of Extinctions.* New York: Touchstone Books, 1996.

Sibley, David Allen. *The Sibley Guide to Birds.* New York: Alfred A. Knopf, 2000.

Smith, Geoffrey R. "Habitat Use and Fidelity in the Striped Plateau Lizard *Sceloporus virgatus,*" *The American Midland Naturalist*, vol. 135, no. 1 (Jan 1996): 68.

Taylor, Richard Cachor. *Hiking Trails and Wilderness Routes of the Chiricahua Mountains.* Tucson: Rainbow Expeditions, 1977.

———. *Location Checklist to the Birds of the Chiricahua Mountains.* Tucson: Borderland Productions, 1997.

———. *Trogons of the Arizona Borderlands.* Tucson: Treasure Chest Publications, 1994.

Terres, John K. *The Audubon Society of North American Birds.* New York: Wings Books, 1991.

about the author

When Ken Lamberton published his first creative nonfiction book *Wilderness and Razor Wire* (Mercury House, 2000), the *San Francisco Chronicle* called it, "entirely original: an edgy, ferocious, subtly complex collection of essays." The book won the 2002 John Burroughs Medal for outstanding nature writing. He has published more than a hundred science and nature articles in many national magazines, and his essays have appeared in literary journals like *Manoa, Northern Lights, Alligator Juniper, Puerto Del Sol,* the *Gettysburg Review,* and David Quammen's anthology *The Best American Science and Nature Writing 2000*

(Houghton Mifflin). He holds degrees in biology and creative writing from the University of Arizona and lives with his wife and daughters in Tucson.

about the photographer

Jeff Garton's photographs have appeared in such magazines as *Arizona Highways, Audubon,* and *Sierra.* He has been the photographer for five books, including *Canyons of Color: Utah's Slickrock Wildlands* with Gary Paul Nabhan (HarperCollins, 1997) and *Grand Canyon: The Great Abyss* with Page Stegner (Thunder Bay Press, 2002). He lives in Tucson.

Library of Congress Cataloging-in-Publication Data
Lamberton, Ken, 1958–
Chiricahua Mountains: bridging the borders of wildness / text by
Ken Lamberton ; photographs by Jeff Garton.
p. cm. — (Desert places)
Includes bibliographical references.
ISBN 0-8165-2290-1 (pbk. : alk. paper)
1. Chiricahua Mountains (Ariz.) — Description and travel.
2. Chiricahua Mountains (Ariz.) — Pictorial works. 3. Natural
history — Arizona — Chiricahua Mountains. I. Garton, Jeff. II. Title.
III. Series.
F817.C5. L36 2003
917.91′53 — dc21
2003005671